THE POWER OF ATTITUDE IN SUCCESS

Enhance Self-belief, Build Success Mindset, Start Thinking Your Way To The Top, And Become The Updated Version Of Yourself.

PRADIP N DAS

Table of Contents

Introduction

Diya got married to Girish and went to live with her husband and mother-in-law. In a very short time, Diya found that she couldn't adjust with her mother-in-law at all as their personalities were different. Diya was angered by many of her mother-in-law's habits. Besides, she criticized Diya constantly. The argument and fighting between Diya and her mother-in-law had increased as time passes and they are at loggerhead throughout the day. All the household anger and despair was causing poor husband's distress. Finally, Diya could not stand her mother-in-law's bad temper and dictatorship any longer, and she decided to do something about it. Diya went to see her father's good friend, uncle Rajesh, who sold herbs. She informed him about the details of her condition and asked if he would give her some poison so that she could solve the problem once and for all.

Uncle Rajesh thought for a while and finally said, "Diya, I will help you solve your problem, but you must listen to me and obey what I tell you." Diya said, "Yes, uncle Rajesh, I will follow whatever you tell me to do." Rajesh uncle went into the back room and returned in a few minutes with a package of herbs. He told Diya, "You cannot use a quick-acting poison to get rid of your mother-in-law, because that would cause people to become suspicious. Therefore, I have given you several herbs that will slowly build up poison in her body. Every other day prepare some special dish and put a little of these herbs in her serving. Now, to make sure that nobody suspects you when she dies, you must be very careful to act very friendly towards her. Never argue with her, obey her every wish, and treat her like a queen." Diya was so happy. She thanked uncle Rajesh and returned home to start as per the advice by uncle Rajesh. Months went by, and every other day, Diya served the specially treated food to her mother-in-law.

She remembered what uncle Rajesh had said about avoiding suspicion, so she controlled her temper, obeyed her mother-in-law, and treated her like her own mother. After six months had passed, the total environment of the household had changed. Diya had practiced controlling her temper so much that she found that she seldom got upset during this period. She had not argued with her mother-in-law, who now seemed much kinder and easier to get along with. The mother-in-law's attitude toward Diya changed, and she began to love Diya like her own daughter. She kept telling friends and relatives that Diya was the best daughter-in-law one could ever find. Diya and her mother-in-law were now treating each other like a real mother and daughter. Girish was very happy to see what was happening. One day, Diya came to see uncle Rajesh and asked for his help again. She said, "Dear uncle Rajesh, please take back the poison. She has changed into such a nice woman, and I love her like my own mother. I do not want her to die because of the poison I gave her." Uncle Rajesh smiled and nodded his head. "Diya, there is nothing to worry about. I never gave you any poison. The herbs I gave you were vitamins to improve her health. The only poison was in your mind and your attitude toward her, but that has been all washed away by the love which you gave to her."

Attitude Has Tremendous Power

Great people like Martin Luther King, Winston Churchill, Nelson Mandela and Mahatma Gandhi always had a purpose in life and had an attitude to sacrifice everything to those purposes. They made all the efforts to accomplish the purpose and had taken all necessary actions to become successful and they became famous in the world. Not only that, you take an example of successful people at any level, you will find their uniqueness in their attitude towards achieving the goal. When attitude takes over, all other elements become trivial. Attitude has the power to shape what is required for a particular goal. Attitude is everything and is the Supreme commander of your mind. If your attitude is right you can achieve anything in life with lesser efforts.

Attitude plays a big role in life. Once attitude is set, you are on the right path—not needing to worry about anything. You will be driven to your destination slowly even without your notice. Then the question arises—what if nobody had the desired attitude? What if someone has problems with attitude? Can somebody correct their attitude or develop the right attitude? What are the things that need to be done to develop the right attitude? How do you monitor your attitude? Which factors play the role in creating an attitude? How do you identify a bad attitude and so on? You can get the answer to all these questions here in this book.

Before you begin to improve your attitude, you must understand how important your life is and how your attitude influences every aspect of your life. You should also realize that a healthy attitude is vital in life to ensure the continued motivation toward your goal.

When a problem surfaces, a winning attitude sees it as a challenge to be solved and not a failure to be ignored. If you have a winning attitude, you will enjoy healthier, more vibrant days. You will have more energy to do the things you love doing the most. A positive attitude can also help you recover from illness in less time. Remember, a healthy attitude delivers a healthy body.

The greatest obstacle toward achieving success in your life is the inability to believe that success is possible. Many do not have a complete sense of their belief, what they can or can't achieve. They cannot see the greatness within, nor do they believe they can achieve whatever they put their minds to. This is a major reason that they do not set goals, for they do not believe they will ever achieve them. Their attitude affects their self-esteem.

"Attitude is little things that make a difference"–*Winston Churchill*

John used to think that something was wrong with him. In school, although he studied well, he was low in confidence, feeble in structure, often seemed to be simpleminded. He developed a belief that he saw himself as a simply stupid guy, that couldn't match others—no particular skill, no winning thinking patterns, no passion. He passed his entire school education like this—the only thing he did was a little bit of study. His school friends laughed at him. They used to go to the movies, hanged out with each other, bunged classes and enjoyed every bit of a student's life. John used to feel inferiority complex often and had become lonely and introverted.

He went to one of the best universities. He didn't fit in there either because of his inferiority complex and introverted nature. Inferiority complex continued to take over his mind. He stayed alone and didn't get along with his classmates. He felt broken from inside. Then something happened. His senior, who was also his roommate in the dorm, realized his problem and told him to read the book "You can win" by Shiv Kheda. That was the ignition point. He obeyed his senior's advice and started reading the book. Once he had completed the book, he kept on telling himself that he can't live the life he is living now, he has to do something and prove himself. He started working on his weaknesses, learning new things every day. Slowly, he became a changed person—he got his confidence back, came out of his inferiority complex, and transformed himself completely. This happened because he changed his attitude toward life.

Elements of Attitude

Attitude has many elements, but the most common and high impact on success is self-belief, willingness to make sacrifices, be out of your comfort zone, action oriented, practicing perseverance, taking ownership, creating good habits, commitment toward the goal and gratitude. These elements are very important in everybody's life and are explained elaborately in the subsequent chapters and provided solutions to improve upon.

Change Your Attitude, Change Your Destiny

According to Zig Ziglar, American author, and motivational speaker, "It is your attitude, not your aptitude that determines your altitude." Our attitude plays a big part in our day to day lives and can affect how our life may turn out in the future. If you have a good attitude, you will be the kind of person who works hard, is a believer in the fact that life is for living, and you will live the kind of life many would aspire to. On the other hand, if you decide to live with a negative attitude, always expecting the worst and never enjoying what you already have in your life, you will find that your inner choices will reflect on the outside.

When you talk about attitude, it comes down to a choice—it is in your hand to choose to have a good attitude or bad attitude in yourself. No other things do matter.

Methods To Improve Attitude

1. Take Action

Appropriate action at right time is the best thing for you to improve your attitude. Worrying is a complete waste of your time, if it is going to happen, it will happen anyway, whether you worry about it or not!

2. Surround Yourself With Good People

Tony Robbins said, "If we surround ourselves with people who are successful, who are forward-moving, who are positive, who are focused on producing results, who support us, it will challenge us to be more and do more and share more. If you can surround yourself with people who will never let you settle for less than you can be, you have the greatest gift that anyone can hope for." The people you surround yourself with most of the time will reflect upon you and your life. So always make sure that these people share your positive vibe, and lift you rather than bring you down. Even more important is to have good, positive people on hand to encourage, support, and inspire us.

3. Forgive Others

Forgiveness means different things to different people. Generally, it involves a decision to let go of resentment and thoughts of revenge. When we get disappointed by other people's actions or non-action, we often get angry. The best way to improve the situation and to improve your attitude is to forgive. Most people do not understand why they do the things they do or say the things they say. Forgiving others or yourself is a difficult thing to do. A forgiving attitude toward someone does not mean that the action the other person did was right. You are forgiving the person, not the action. Forgiveness benefits you more than the other person. By your forgiveness, you will improve your attitude. Holding on to grudges will only cause you more harm than good.

4. Act With A Purpose

To achieve success and fulfillment, action must start with the vision. When you take action, always take steps to act with a purpose, so that your actions are in line with your values. Many people just live life with no real reason for what they do and why they are doing it. Instead, always live with a sense of purpose, so that when you live your life, you will be able to know the effect on you and those around you.

5. Be Polite

Politeness helps to improve your relationships with others, helps to build rapport, boost your self-esteem and confidence, and improves your communication skills. So, if you want to improve your attitude, always use words such as "Please," "Thank you," etc. every single time you are given the opportunity. When you are nice to someone who is helping you out or when you need some assistance, you will find that you will get more when you are polite, but very often we forget these simple words.

Finally, no matter how simple it sounds, having a positive and friendly attitude will open new doors and opportunities for you. Politeness is contagious and it can change your and someone else's life.

6. Avoid Comparison With Others

It is very difficult not to compare yourself with others in modern life. If we start examining our achievements and accomplishments, then we can raise the bar even further. But if you want to improve your attitude to life and those around you, then stop comparing yourself to others. When you compare, you think someone else's life looks better than yours. It is important to remember that you are only observing the external view; you cannot compare the internal view. Therefore, you should only focus on your own life and attitude to it and you will be much happier in the process.

7. Hope For The Best

Every situation offers a learning opportunity and an outlet to become better in the long-run. There are ample examples of people making it through hard times and coming out polished and more complete than they ever were before. When life is hectic, we tend to focus on what could go wrong in our lives rather than focusing on what could go right. Hope unites us as humans during challenging situations and traumatic events. Hope fuels passion, inner drive, inspiration, and energizes us to push ourselves to new limits. To improve this attitude, you can try not to complain for seven days and instead replace any negative thoughts with a positive one. Expect the very best out of every situation and see the improvement in your attitude.

8. Live In The Present Moment.

Living in the present moment means no longer thinking about what happened in the past and not worrying about what will happen in the future. It means living today in the present moment and the only important moment is the present moment.

In order to live in the present moment utterly, instead of rushing about, try to spend time perceiving your thoughts and becoming more mindful of your self-talk. Anxiety, stress, and worry are all signs you are not living in the present. To improve your attitude, learn how to take a break, to sit and be quiet even if it is just for ten minutes a day.

9. Being Grateful For Everything You Have

Being grateful for everything we have in life is beneficial for us in many ways because gratefulness is one of the most powerful attitudes to have in life. The book has a full chapter for this. In short, if you wish to have a better life, give thanks for all that you have each day. When you rise early, practice grace before you do anything. This kind of practice will set your day off nicely, your attitude will improve.

"If you want life to change, you have to change. If you want life to be better, you have to be better"—Jim Rohn

Chapter Summary

In a nutshell, attitude can have a big impact on success and failure in life. There are many ways a person can improve attitude or practice a positive attitude.

"If you don't like something, change it. If you can't change it, change your attitude."
—*Maya Angelou*

An ambitious young boy once asked his coach about the secret of success. Coach asked him to meet him near the river the next morning. The young boy came near the river the next morning. Coach asked the young boy to walk with him toward the river. When the water got up to their neck, the coach took the young boy by surprise and ducked him into the water. The young boy struggled to get out but his coach was strong and kept him there until the boy started to turn blue. Just then, the coach pulled his head out of the water and the first thing the young boy did was to gasp a deep breath of air. Coach asked him, "What did you want most when you were there inside the river?"

The young boy replied, "Air." The Coach said, "That is the secret of success. When you want success as badly as you wanted the air, then you will get it. There is no other secret."

What Is Attitude?

Attitude is the way of looking at life, the way you choose to see and respond to events, situations, people, and yourself. Your attitude is not something that happens to you, your attitude is your choice. Your attitude is created by the thoughts you choose. You decide how you will perceive and process the events of life and work. You are the architect of your mind. You decide if your mindset is positive or negative. If you want to feel better you have to think better. To be positive, it is necessary to be disciplined in your thinking.

Your mind has enormous power. The performance begins with your thoughts.

Indeed, your mind is your most important resource center. How you see and respond to the events of life is shaped by your mindset and patterns of thinking. Therefore, an essential key to success is to train your mind and use it wisely.

Though life sometimes is very complex and hard. Different people respond to the same situation in different ways. It all depends on the attitude of the person such as temperament, education, prior experience, upbringing, mindset, etc. For example, when it is raining, someone will go out and enjoy dancing or catching raindrops, while someone will be disappointed or could not enjoy at the park.

Positive Attitude And Success

The one common attribute that every successful person has is the power of positivity. By creating positive energy around yourself, you can bring positive changes to your personal and professional life. Success starts from the thought process, so we need to train our thoughts to attain success. By having a positive attitude towards everything and believing in all your capabilities, you can easily attain success in life. To succeed, you need to set goals that are both short-term and long-term. Once these goals are in place, make an action plan to achieve them. A positive attitude along with hard work and perseverance is how you will achieve your goals. Keeping positivity in your mindset is the way to achieve these goals. Besides, when good thoughts generate in the mind then it also helps in boosting our confidence. Sometimes, at the time of making an important decision in life, people may find it hard to determine the right path due to stress and tension. By having a positive attitude, they can put the right amount of thoughts which may help them in taking the right decision. Working with a positive attitude will only benefit the process.

Positive Attitude And Health

Attitude directly has an impact on health. Positive thinking helps in managing stress management and can even improve your health. The person with a positive attitude approaches the problem as a personal challenge rather than as hopeless. A negative attitude often causes physical ailments and generates less productivity. Just like diseases, a positive attitude is contagious and infectious. A positive attitude can have key health benefits such as increased life span, lower rates of depression, better psychological and physical well-being, better cardiovascular health, etc.

Positive Attitude And Relationships

A positive attitude can boost your relationships. It can improve personal relationships as well as organizational relationships. Carrying a positive assertiveness is very important when it comes to success. When nurturing a relationship with a client, it is very important to listen to the needs of your client and keep an upbeat approach. People intuitively respond to your attitude and mood. Being confident in your abilities and prioritizing the needs of the clients is a formula for success.

Positive Attitude And Team Work

A positive attitude directly affects teamwork. In any teamwork, you should always try to stay away from negative people. When the team is filled with positivity, members feel more energized and confident; they demonstrate a higher level of relationship for the benefits of the team and one another. Their individual as well as team performance reach higher levels. To bring positivity to the teamwork, nobody should blame or accuse or point fingers at other team members for any issues that occur. Instead, team members should create a mindset to help colleagues to solve their problems and cooperate. Everyone should understand that their role is crucial. A helpful attitude along with a willingness to help others to achieve a goal makes a strong team.

A positive attitude helps you to cope up with the daily affairs of life more easily. It brings optimism into life and helps to avoid worries and negative thinking. If you bring positivity to your life and make constructive changes, you will be happier, brighter, and more successful. It is certainly a state of mind that is well worth developing.

Chapter Summary

By filling positivity in life, one can reach any heights of happiness and success and can become successful in personal life as well as professional. A positive person is happier and healthier than other people who do not have a positive outlook on life.

Once, the team manager was talking about tactics with the player of the team before a crucial final match. A player interrupted him and said that he thought that the strategy was a waste of time. "The God has already decided who will win." he proclaimed.

"Do you mean that fate has decided the result in advance?" The team manager asked.

"Yes, I am." the player responded.

The team manager took a coin out of his pocket and said, "So if I toss this coin and it comes up heads, we win, but if it is tails we lose. Is that how fate works?"

"Pretty much." said the player.

The team manager tossed the coin and it came up heads.

"See, God has decided. We cannot lose now!"

They went to play with the positive thoughts in the final match with renewed enthusiasm.

After a glorious victory, the players met with the team manager to celebrate.

"Do you believe in fate now?" the team manager was asked.

The manager smiled, reached into his pocket, and pulled out the coin to show to the others.

It was heads on both sides.

"No, I do not believe in fate, just the value of self-belief. When the players thought that we could not lose, I knew that we could not lose."

Sometimes, we think that the script has already been written and that success is for a chosen few.

I share this adapted story to encourage you to believe in yourself, to have confidence in your abilities, and to launch yourself into the fray with energy and enthusiasm. If you do, you will win many great victories.

What Is Self-Belief?

Everyone desires success but it does not come to everybody. The most important thing which makes the difference between a successful and unsuccessful person is whether they believe in themselves or not. Successful people are more determined about their goals, and they try to make the best out of every positive opportunity which comes to them in any situation.

Many factors contribute to success but one of the most important factors is self-belief. The achievement of a person mostly depends on how strong his self-belief is.

Many times, the difference in whether you succeed or not comes down to one simple thing, i.e. self-belief. Every human being has strengths and weaknesses but our mind is most inclined to the weaknesses or negativities such as anxiety, problems or difficulties instead of choosing to believe in our natural ability to overcome the challenges.

Self-belief is how much a person believes in himself. This is very important because it builds a person's self. Self-belief comprises values, skills, knowledge, and abilities. A person without self-belief constantly downplays their abilities and in most cases, they achieve less because they do not believe that they could have done better. On the other hand, a person with self-belief knows their worth and value.

For instance, when people with no self-belief or are low in self-belief see a job opportunity with the skills they possess, they may act half-heartedly because they believe that they are not good enough for the job. People with self-belief, on the other hand, will pursue the job whole-heartedly because they believe that they are well-qualified for the job.

In the end, people without self-belief or self-confidence may end up working a much lower job category than what they deserve. Meanwhile, people with self-belief will move from that job to a better one and might eventually reach a much higher level.

This small example indicates that while self-belief might seem inconsequential or very insignificant, but it can adversely affect our entire lives both directly and indirectly.

Impacts Of Self-Belief In Success

People often set goals in their minds, and just keep them to one side, pushing back the commence date to pursue them for one reason after another. Those who have self-belief, on the other hand, have the support of cognitive biases that allow them to look at a challenge and believe that they might have the capabilities to accomplish it, rather than becoming consumed by self-doubt. People do not put best efforts when they do not believe that they can do something and without best efforts, the chances of successfully achieving a goal are greatly impaired. Self-belief has many benefits that contributed to the success.

1. Increases Confidence

You need to be confident to succeed and should be able to handle all the challenges in the way to success. With a lack of self-belief, you will lose confidence in you and will not be able to handle the task properly. On the other hand, when you believe in yourself, you gain confidence that ultimately helps to get success. You might fail many times, but you will not lose confidence. You will learn from the failure and will strive towards achieving your goal. A successful people always have a strong belief in themselves. When you believe that you can achieve something, the task becomes always easier to do.

2. Improves Focus

People who believe in themselves are more likely to achieve more because believing in themselves made people stick to their goals. Even in the time of immense difficulties or challenges, they keep on focused and find out the path by which they can reach their goals. Their self-belief increases their willpower, so they relentlessly work hard to achieve their goals. Many people are unsuccessful because they give up when they face obstacles due to a lack of self-belief. In short, people who get over all obstacles by focusing on their goals, and they are those who are successful in their life.

3. Assists To Explore The Opportunities

Lack of self-belief makes you blind whereas self-belief opens your mind and you will find various ways and means to go forward or to tackle situation which ultimately helps you to achieve your goals. When you have clear goals and a strong belief in yourself, your mind has the highest possibility to explore the opportunities in and around you. Self-belief makes a person relaxed and helps to think out of the box and find creative solutions that bring success. Once a person develops self-belief, the only thing that separates them from their goal and destination is time and hard work. Believing in yourself will make you see the best outcome and work towards it.

Ways To Improve Self-Belief

When Thomas Alva Edison successfully invented the light bulb, all his colleagues and assistants were very happy with such great success. Edison called one office boy and asked him to test that bulb. He was very nervous to even hold that bulb in his hand. He was so shaky holding it that due to nervousness, the bulb was dropped from his hand accidentally. The office boy was scared that he would get fired from his job for dropping such an important invention. After two days Edison again asked that office boy to test the bulb which he constructed. All assistants were surprised and said, "Why did you call him again? There are chances of him dropping it again." Edison replied, "It took me one day to construct that bulb again, and even if he drops it again, I can construct another bulb within a day. But if

I do not give him the same task again then he would have lost his self-belief and confidence which would be very difficult to get back and I do not want that to happen."

Self-belief can be improved in many ways. There are various tools and techniques available to improve self-belief. One has to practice these with due diligence because it is a gradual process but when a person does it with discipline, improvement happens in self-belief. Fortunately, believing in yourself is a learnable skill but it required time to acquire that skill. Always remember that nothing will work if you do not believe in yourself.

Everyone can improve themselves and do better in their life. The more they believe that they can do better, the more they try to expand their horizon and push themselves to improve. If you believe, you can gain knowledge, experience, and acquired skills to become a better person. On the other hand, if you cannot believe to do better, then it is hard to make any progress. Your values in life influence the belief about yourself and the world around you to a great extent. When you believe in yourself and chose to be a good person you will find yourself to be more positive and successful in life.

There are many ways to develop self-belief.

- Lack of self-belief has two main reasons: self-doubt and low self-esteem. To get rid of this, you need to ask questions such as: "What do you want? What is your goal? What is bothering you? What makes you afraid? What can you do to overcome this?" Finding answers to these questions will be the first step to rebuild your self-belief. During the process, you should be conscious to work towards your goals and to push away the low self-esteem. Therefore, you need to give yourself the space to do self-talk on all the things you would like to achieve and reaffirm your belief every day.

- Visualization is a strong tool that reinforces your belief in yourself because this influences our behavior. If you see yourself as one of the best chess players in the world, or you see yourself as the future Olympic gold medalist in any sports, you will start behaving like that. So, you need to see yourself as someone worthy and amazing. Visualization can help you create that image.

You can make a few affirmations such as you are the future gold medalist or future champion, you are working on that, making efforts to improve yourself to that level. If you visualize the process everyday and affirm yourself, you will surely improve your self-belief.

- Supporting others, even your friends and family members will help you to develop your self-belief. You should start giving people authentic positive feedback, this will help to grow their self-belief and help you to reap the benefits of being part of a motivated group.

- Fear ruins the self-belief from inside. The roots of each fear are specific to them. Exploring reasons and sources can help us to address roots, and can assist in weeding it out of our brains and allowing space for self-belief to grow.

Fear of failure is preventing most people to take initiative and to face challenges. People give up before taking challenges only thinking of fear of failure. One effective way to develop self-belief is by facing your fears. Once you face and conquer your fears, self-belief will automatically improve.

- To develop your self-belief, you need to take care of yourself physically. Physical care can directly influence your mental and emotional health, so everybody should do physical exercise regularly. Looking good and feeling good will surely help boost your self-confidence. According to psychologists, taking care of your mind, body, and spirituality raises

the level of dopamine in your
brain which is responsible for
improving your tenacity.

- Practicing mindfulness can help
  you hear yourself and how you
  talk to yourself. Whenever you
  notice negative self-talk in
  yourself, just stop, consider it,
  evaluate its truth, and try out a
  neutral or positive alternative.

Chapter Summary

Self-belief is indeed the first step to
success. Once self-belief is improved, all
other things are aligned automatically. In
this chapter, we have learned what self-
belief is, the impact of self-belief in success,
and how it can be improved. Finally, self-
belief motivates people to explore their
potentials and this motivation may lead to
the achievement of goals and aspirations.

"Great success requires greater sacrifice."—
Sachin Srabhu

Real Success is never made without any sacrifices. You will be surprised to know that Elon Musk worked from early morning until late evening. During early in his career, he lived in the same warehouse where he rented his office, and when he needed to take a shower he would use the locker rooms of a local stadium. At the early stages of an entrepreneur, social life is nonexistent. Bill Gates wrote in a blog post in December 2018 that he stopped listening to music and watching TV in his twenties. He did it because he thought they would just distract him from thinking about the software. That blackout period lasted about five years.

Take the example of great people like Steve Jobs, Oprah Winfrey, or anyone really who has made it to the very pinnacle of success. When they finally obtained their greatest accolades, in their speeches they often talked about what they gave up to achieve their dreams or how much the people around them had to sacrifice. They all have stories of giving up on certain things in order to achieve something greater. Much of this sacrifice has to do with how they spent their time. Sacrifice is centered on time. When one sacrifices for something that can reward them in the future, they can put the time in their favor.

One should be ready to pay the price for success. To build an empire, one needs to invest enormous amounts of time in reading, learning, and experimenting.

You will be inspired to know what changes occur in the mind of the person when they make a sacrifice. When sacrifices are made, the level of grit and determination increases to a manifold and there are a lot of things that are at stake. People have no other option but to focus on the work for achieving the goals—at this point, people make all efforts and put all resources toward achieving that. Thereby, sacrifices are directly proportional to improvement in determination, will, power, focus, hard work, discipline, and many more actions required for making it all happen— willingness to sacrifice directly determines your level of success. If you truly want to reach another level of success in any area of your life, you will need to make extraordinary sacrifices to reach there. Sacrifices can be in the form of time, money, resources, enjoyment, sleep, etc. Parents sacrifice everything for their children, in some cases, they even sacrifice their precious time and career for supporting a child. These sacrifices are essential for success. A successful career requires dedication and if people are not willing to make sacrifices in life for their career, for their future, then they never reach that success.

Every individual in this world wants to achieve success and luxurious life but wanting success will not guarantee a successful life. There's a huge difference between successful people and unsuccessful people—successful people know that anything worth never comes easy, success is not as easy as unsuccessful people think. Successful people know that when you want something from life then you need to sacrifice something for it.

The biggest problem of unsuccessful people is that they want to succeed but they want it without doing anything or without moving out of their comfort zone. While successful people get success because they work hard for it, they sacrifice a lot for that success. Success needs Sacrifice means life demands something in return to give you success.

Success is something that you earn, something you must achieve by your hard work after a lot of sacrifices.

Sacrifice Of Comforts

Needless to say that people who wish to get success in their comfort zone, actually never want their dream to come true. Comfort zone is a nice place, the best place, but nothing ever grows there. If you want to be successful, if you crave for abundance—if you find success as important as oxygen—than you will never settle yourself in a comfort zone. Successful people take risks, move out of their comfort zones, take every possible step to get what they want; successful people go above their limits, hence to be successful you need to sacrifice your comfort zone.

To function effectively in this rapidly changing world, you need to learn new things to remain valuable. Continuous lifelong learning will help you to adapt to all changes. When you are always learning, you will more easily step out of your comfort zone and will grow in your career. Besides, learning new things gives you a feeling of accomplishment which, in turn, boosts your confidence in your capabilities. You feel more ready to take on challenges and succeed.

Sacrifices Of Social Life

Many people, to become successful, have gone far away from social life. For some people, it is not so difficult to sacrifice social life, but for an extrovert it is the hardest thing.

Sacrifices in social life do not mean that you will be completely detached from social life. You can keep in touch with your close friends and family from time to time, but completely away from those regular evening dinners and weekends with friends and other socializing which consume your time and distract you from your goal.

Sacrifices Of Entertainment

Whether your hobby is playing guitar, traveling, or social networking, if it takes up too much of your time and distracts you from your goal, then you have to let them go, at least for time being. Now if your hobby is one of those things that is a stress reliever after a long week of work, that is fine, but if you are out playing golf every day in the evening, that is unacceptable in these circumstances. Think of it this way—it is always a better choice to sacrifice today's fun for tomorrow's freedom.

Sacrifices Of Family

There are several examples where people have sacrificed their families to achieve their goals and dreams. Sometimes, family members face too much distress because of this. But the bigger the sacrifices, the bigger the success.

Chapter Summary

In a nutshell, your willingness to sacrifice directly determines your level of success—if you only make small sacrifices, you will only ever achieve small success; if you want to achieve an enormous goal such as a World-class chess player, you need to make enormous sacrifices. Sacrifice is hard—no one said it would be easy—but every enormous success requires enormous sacrifice.

"Great achievement is usually born of great sacrifice, and is never the result of selfishness."— Napoleon Hill

"The greatest glory in living lies not in falling, but in rising every time you fall."—Nelson Mandela

There was a king who was looking for the right man to marry his daughter. So he decided to set a challenge to pick the person who will not give up at the first sign of hard times and who has the right mindset. To pass the challenge, participants had to wear the royal metal armor and climb 500 stairs to the top of the mountain where the king's castle was located. Many strong men from around the world came to take on the challenge. But once they put on the armor, they realized that it will be an impossible task. Most men took the first step, then they looked up at the remaining 499 steps and gave up. A couple of men managed to get to the second step but then decided to concede defeat. This went on for the next couple of hundred men, some making it even to the third step.

The king was looking worried. He wondered if there was any person worthy of his daughter. Everyone has failed so far and they were talking that the challenge was set up so it could not be completed—the strongest military men tried and failed; the best athletes tried and failed; the hardest working men tried and failed to get past the third stairs—no one was able to make it any further. They all blamed the armor and the steps. If only the armor was lighter if only the stairs would not be so steep.

And then to the surprise of everyone, a young man, that did not look special, said he wanted to try. He put on the heavy armor and went towards the steps. Everyone yelled he would not be able to get past the first step. But he made to the second in no-time. When he came to the fourth step he could barely lift his shaking feet. But he took a deep breath and made the next step. Now he felt like he was about to drop, but he decided to push on. He kept repeating to himself, "One step at a time. I just need to make this one."

As he got to the fifth step, he suddenly felt a huge pull from the top. Suddenly his armor was a little bit lighter. So he decided to make one more step saying to himself "I am not ready to give up yet". To his surprise, on this next step, the armor felt lighter. He felt very tired but thought he can make one more step and this way the ordinary young man continued. With each step, he felt his armor getting lighter and his goal closer.

When the young man completed this challenge the king first congratulated him and then shared with him a secret about the challenge, "You see the point of the challenge was to make sure that the man who is going to marry my daughter would not be the kind of man that would give up at the first couple of tough moments. The armor represents the tough moments and the magnet on top that made each step easier after the couple few you had to make on your own represented the willpower and experience that will make your future endeavors easier to bear. Because with the right kind of person by your side and with the right kind of mindset and focus you can achieve anything no matter the weight of the problem. So now you know that the hard part in every situation you two will face in the future are the first couple of steps and then it will get easier. You have proved yourself and can now marry my daughter. [1]

Success comes with hard work and perseverance. Remember, in childhood a lazy student can seldom achieve good grades. If you are not prepared to work hard you should not expect good results.

America's famous president Abraham Lincoln was born in a log cabin in the forest.

---

[1] *Reference : https://purposefocuscommitment.com/perseverance-story-kings-challenge-give-up-too-quickly*

He could not afford a lamp and read borrowed books with the light of the fire in the hearth. He was self-educated and merely by working hard, he rose to be the greatest man of his time. All great achievers of mankind such as Newton, Leonardo Da Vinci, Einstein, Addison, Mahatma Gandhi, Dr. Abdul Kalam, Leon Musk, etc. worked very patiently and perseveringly in their chosen fields.

What Is Perseverance?

In short, perseverance is to keep on going during setbacks and challenges. It is the inner call of a human being to continue in the game when the entire environment says it's time to quit. It is just resolving to one foot after another when the finish line is nowhere in sight. Perseverance is a series of bridges for crossing the rivers of adversity as you pursue your vision and success.

Why Perseverance?

When a kid learns to stand up and tries to walk, he falls again and again. By nature and instinct, he gets up, and again tries to step forward, and he falls again. But finally, he succeeded in walking. The same thing happened to each one of us when we were kids.

Perseverance is one of the key secrets and the root cause of success. A person who is not so talented or not having much knowledge can be successful in life only with perseverance. On the other hand, a highly intelligent person or genius but is lethargic and reluctant to diligence, can hardly prosper in life because all great things have been made or constructed only by perseverance.

When we were kids, we were guided by perseverance. But as we grow, this instinct vanishes or is reduced to a greater extent. Many people crumble or give up in case of repeated failures. But a man having perseverance does not admit his defeat. He tries again and again and finally attains success. A persevering person is one who has tremendous self-confidence, resolution, untiring energy and is determined to continue till the end.

In human life, perseverance plays a very important role. Michael Phelps, the greatest swimmer could not have won 15 Gold medals in Olympic and could not have created history, if he had not been working hard during days and nights over the years with tremendous perseverance. Had he not been persevering, Usain Bolt could not become the World's fastest sprinter by winning three gold medals in three consecutive Olympics. There are so many examples of perseverance.

Practicing Perseverance

Many people practice perseverance for short period—their journey ends by giving up after trying for some time. But for successful people, the period is longer, over several years or even decades. These are painful and testing moments where no matter how much effort you put in the journey, there is hardly any positive movement. Naturally, you will get discouraged thinking about what is going on; even more, frustrating when you find out others around you are making good progress on their goals. But the question arises—how to keep on going? How to motivate ourselves when we get very thirsty by walking in the desert and there is no water in sight?

Always remember that most successful people have endured hardships, challenges, and failures at some point in their life. They kept going because they kept their purpose and goals in mind, so they were determined to make a difference in both their lives and those of others.

How To Improve Perseverance?

- Perseverance is nothing but habit and mental attitude which requires mental toughness to translate your desires into actions. Grit and determination play a vital role in perseverance. To deal with discouragement, you need to keep reminding yourself of your big dream and vision of why you decided to pursue this journey.

- Perseverance requires focusing on your skills, knowledge and abilities. To get success, you need to keep on honing your skills, upgrading your knowledge, and improving your abilities.

- Action is what makes your dreams come true, translates plans into results. Sustained action is what separates winners from losers.

- You should always remind yourself of the rewards of achieving success to diminish the thinking of the adverse consequences of failing. You need to practice your mind to view struggle as a gateway to victory. You should make a habit to celebrate your small wins or achievements along the way. You keep on visualizing how good it will feel to finally succeed and let these good feelings motivate you. In the end, victory is sweeter after conquering challenges.

- You should read the biographies of successful people who achieved great successes despite huge obstacles, setbacks, and failures they encountered. Autobiographies of Helen Keller, Ludwig Van Beethoven, Thomas Edison, Terry Fox, and many others provide motivating examples.

- You should not allow to let your mind run wild with imagined failures; rather excite it with anticipated victories. You cannot persist if you have a gloomy outlook on the future and feel depressed. You should practice switching your mind to optimism and hopefulness by self-awareness and self-management.

- A journey of one thousand miles begins with one step. No matter how daunting the task is, just take the first step, and keep on moving one step after another. The journey is no less important than the destination.

- You should always be around people who would support and encourage you to achieve your goals. You should take advices of the experts to fulfill your dreams. You should talk to, open up, and share your feelings. Sometimes just a simple discussion on the subject stimulates brainstorming for solutions and ideas around. It is necessary to surround yourself with a network of supporters including family, friends, colleagues, and neighbors to support you, encourage you, and cheer you on towards the finish line.

Chapter Summary

As per Jim Watkins, "A river cuts through a rock not because of its power, but because of its persistence." Therefore, perseverance must be practiced from the very childhood so that this becomes a habit and become a part and parcel of one's life. By practicing this, a person can work easily on the turbulent sea of his life's journey. Great men of the world were born in cottages but they died in palaces. Hence, not poverty but idleness is a great curse. To conclude, success will surely come to those who work hard and who work untiringly without losing enthusiasm.

"If you can't fly then run if you can't run then walk if you can't walk then crawl, but whatever you do, you have to keep moving forward."—Martin Luther King.

"Action is the Foundational Key to All Success."—Pablo Picasso

This means that to get anything done, you have to do something about it. Dreaming and hoping will not get you the success you are looking for. Fundamental Action has to take place to create success in your life. Change does not simply come from analysis. It only comes from action. It is never easy and requires determination and discipline.

Success in anything starts with action. Timely action taking should be a part of our habit. You will find many people who have dreams and goals but do not do anything to accomplish. For any dreams to accomplish, you need a take a series of actions, built with planning. If you plan properly and act accordingly, you can attain any height. To make action taking a habit, you need to start with small actions. Then, once you complete that action, try another small action. Soon those little actions will add up and will make your foundational key for success.

Why Actions Are So Important?

Be it Leon Musk, Mukesh Ambani, or Alibaba, one thing is common—they never delay in taking action. Whatever good things they learn or come to their mind, they immediately implement it. If you do not take action, the idea will die or learning will be replaced with another new learning, ultimately, opportunity will be lost. Dreaming is important to get the drive to do things, but ultimately you need to execute that. Execution is the key to convert the idea to the desired outcome. Action-oriented people never fail. The habit of taking action is the key to success. It is as simple as if you want to learn to drive, you can learn the process by reading books on driving, or watching videos, or listening to a driver but you will never learn to drive until you execute all that knowledge by actually starting to drive.

Reading is a great first step to making the necessary changes in your life, however, the changes can only be possible once you take action. If you keep on reading and you do not take any action on your learning, it is nothing but procrastination. Always remember that success and procrastination are not friends.

It is important to understand that change and success is an ongoing process. You cannot try once or make just one attempt and decide to quit. If you keep on taking action, it turns into habitual patterns of behavior. The hardest part about taking action towards change is getting started. The sooner you start and the more you practice this action, the more natural it becomes, and taking action will slowly become a habit.

How to become more action-oriented in life:

1. Monitor Time

Pay attention to how you are spending every minute of your day. Time cannot be paused, it passes very fast. A person cannot be action-oriented if he or she does not keep track of time. Every minute counts. Plan properly, but it should not end up with an endless game. Time management is necessary. Do not over-plan or overthink. It should be more of brainstorming for you.

2. Be Impatient

If you want to be action-oriented, you have to be inquisitive. Being impatient sometimes is just fine. If you are curious to know the results, they will lead you to be more active. But for this, you need to sharpen your curiosity and urgency.

3. Visualize

When you set your goal and want to achieve something big in life, practice visualizing yourself in that position. This creates an urge or desire to take action to reach there. Your mental picture of yourself has a powerful effect on your behavior—picturing yourself to be the person you want to pave the path for, can help you to be an action-oriented individual. Actions in your life begin with improvements in your internal mental pictures.

4. Become Risk Lover

The Wright brothers would have never made the airplane if they had paid attention to the naysayers. Henry Ford would have never invented the automobile if he had listened to his critics. The list goes on and on. Every breakthrough in history, be it in business, science, medicine, sports, etc., is the result of an individual who took a risk and refused to play it safe. Successful people understand this. They invent, achieve, surpass, and succeed because they dare to live beyond the realm of normal.

Most of the successful people in the world are risk-takers. They take many risks in their way to achieve success. Their grit and determination increased many folds by taking a risk to make that work happen. To climb the ladder of success, you must be actively involved and must be willing to take the risk.

5. Improve Self-Confidence

Self-confidence is the biggest secret of success. Those who have confidence in themselves, will surely become action-oriented and achieve success. People with a high level of self-confidence achieve their desired goals in life and attain success while those lacking confidence and self-belief are perennial underachievers. Lack of confidence results in inaction and not standing up for oneself.

6. Accept Failures

Failure is part of life and the pillar of success. If you do not fail, you can never taste success. You may break down many times during failures, but never give up. Learn from the mistakes and try not to repeat them. Failure increases stubbornness and becomes more action-oriented persons.

7. Practice Discipline

A disciplined person is more action-oriented. Being lethargic is a deadly weapon, not only killing valuable time but wasting opportunities that may come your way. Set tasks for yourself and complete them accordingly.

8. Reward Yourself

Rewarding yourself is one way of motivating yourself. When you complete work within the timeline set by you, you should reward yourself in whatever way you want. But, if you complete a task at the eleventh hour, or just manage to finish on time, you should refrain from celebrating. This will transmit a message to your brain to be more action-oriented in the future.

Chapter Summary

To achieve anything, you have to do something about it. Every one of us has our own goals and dreams but only a few have the drive to act towards these goals and dreams. If you want to achieve the things you want to achieve, then you have to be action-oriented.

"In order to carry a positive action we must develop here a positive vision."—Dalai Lama

"Everything changes for the better when you take ownership of your own problems."— *Robert Ringer*

I remember when I first entered into the professional world, I was always very much hesitant to take ownership, always do the routine work what most other people were doing. Initially, I had a fear in my mind what others will say. Later I understood that by taking ownership of any activities, you are not only empowering yourself but you are improving your productivity also. With this, your authority increases automatically and a message goes to the other team members, be it your seniors, colleagues, or juniors. Slowly, you start realizing that you are the captain of the ship, all others are just the passengers—your value in the organization increases and that impacts your career and the organization too. A simple question—will you take enough care of a rented car or rented house? Only when you own a house or a car or anything, you start taking extra care. Mark Twain rightly said, "Almost any man worthy of his salt would fight to defend his home, but no one ever heard of a man going to war for his boarding house."

Ownership is the mentality that stimulates and causes enthusiasm. Ownership is a feeling, it cannot be delegated. An ownership mindset is the willingness to think big and deliver better and in a manner that adds to one's reputation.

Always remember that you are the only one in charge of your career, nobody else. Ultimately, it all comes down to you and your overall approach towards your work, goal and life. How much control you take in your life and how many actions you display will ultimately decide your success or failure. How badly you want to achieve your goal and how committed you are. Commitment leads to career ownership and career ownership leads to success.

How It Influence In Success

Take the example of any successful person, be your coach, your friend or a legend, or a sports person, ownership is very common to all of them. They used to always take ownership that helps them to grow continuously and become successful. Ownership creates leverage in the career and in life as taking ownership results in huge wins for yourself throughout your life. It makes a big difference in shaping your career and your success. Ownership means delivering a continuous improvement of your performance, as opposed to being complacent and sticking to the status quo, just because that is what was done in the past.

How To Improve Ownership

1. Take Initiative

Taking initiative is the first sign of taking ownership. No one will ever prevent you from taking the extra steps to accomplish your goals. Taking initiative means stepping up to the plate to make something great happen. Competition in today's business world is fierce. If you don't take the initiative to differentiate yourself from this competition, you will be left behind.

2. Commitment

Commitment towards your goals with true passion is the key to what you intend to do. A great way to establish commitment and continuous improvement is to set daily goals for yourself. This gives you purpose, drive, ambition, and something to reach for daily. Your daily goals should be actionable and attainable so that at the end of the day, you feel accomplished and can experience that feeling of success. Whether it is developing new creativity or any new learning, you should commit to your role and commit to becoming better than you were yesterday.

3. Become Accountable

The most effective way to build ownership is to take more responsibility and hold yourself accountable for that. Once you start taking responsibility, you will build ownership slowly. Accountability gives people a greater sense of ownership over their work. You can improve ownership by delegating responsibility for functions within your team. When someone feels greater responsibility, they often feel personal pride, making them care more about the quality of their work. This results in improved motivation, enthusiasm, and greater commitment to the team.

4. Try Discomfort

Comfort zones may feel safe, but change never happens there. We need to step outside our comfort zones to grow, develop, and create a successful life.

5. Self-Awareness

Being self-aware is acknowledging that you may not always have the right answers but are always willing to learn. You should always be open to the feedback you receive. While it may feel uncomfortable at the beginning, you are gaining the additional knowledge and the respect of others that will ultimately pave your way towards future success.

6. Remember The End Goal

People who always see the end goal in their mind that drives them to work for the goal, they ultimately achieve the goal. Committing yourself to your goal will get you that much closer to success. By having the end goal in mind, you are essentially creating the road map for your success.

7. Refrain From Blaming

Successful people do not blame anybody or anything in the world when they fail to achieve something. They accept it, learn from their mistakes, and then do something about it. When people make some mistakes or fail to achieve desired results, their minds try to find ways to discharge the psychological pain by projecting the discomfort, anger, or pain onto another person or situation. This process can happen so quickly that we do not even realize it. We forget our role in that situation and fail to take ownership.

In his book "Wooden on Leadership", John Wooden with Steve Jamison said, "You can stumble and fall, make errors and mistakes, but you are not a failure until you start blaming others, including fate, for your results. Always believe there is a positive to be found in the negative. Things usually happen for a reason, even when you are unable to discern the reason. Remember, 'There is a special providence even in the fall of a sparrow.'"

To overcome that you need to observe your thoughts and actions minutely during the adverse situation. Most people tend to immediately blame others. If you hear yourself complaining, take a pause and ask yourself, "What can I learn from this? Can I avoid this?" The best way to stop blaming is self-awareness and empathy. True accountability requires honesty, self-awareness, and a willingness to bear the pain that comes with honestly attributing responsibility.

8. Focus on Solutions

Anthony J. D'Angelo rightly said, *"Focus 90% of your time on solutions and only 10% of your time on problems."*

You need to remember that what you focus on expands. If you focus on problems, you will get more problems. If you focus on solutions, you will get more solutions. Whenever there is any problem, make a list of possible solutions for the problem at hand. Whatever solution comes to your mind, immediately write it down. The essence of capturing solutions and then putting them on paper activates your brain. You start to think of more ways to overcome this problem at hand. Once you have listed all the possible solutions, the next objective is to decide which solution is best. If you think long and hard enough, the solutions are always there. This type of thinking can be a total game-changer for anybody or any organization.

Necessity is, after all, the mother of all invention. So, if something is important to you, whether it be your health, fitness, relationship, career, education, or happiness, you will find a solution even though the problem is very hard.

Chapter Summary

Peter Drucker wisely points out that effective executives must develop character, foresight, self-reliance, and courage. Organizations, he reminds us, are made up of ordinary people who together must do extraordinary things. This is possible only when people take ownership.

"If you want to change the world, start with yourself"—Mahatma Gandhi

Have you ever wondered about the habits of successful people? Maybe they are lucky or were just in the right place at the right time, maybe they are born with something extraordinary or they have come from different planets! There is a certain set of traits that every successful person has in common. If you can understand what some of these traits of successful people are, you too will be able to adopt these practices and finally achieve some of the success and happiness that you have always wanted. The key thing to remember about successful people is that they understand that simply wanting to achieve success is not enough, you have to match this desire with effort, strength of mind, and drive.

Habits Are Very Powerful

Habits shape your life far more than you probably realize. Habits are very strong. Our brains cling to them at the exclusion of all else—including common sense. It is said that more than forty percent of the actions a person performs each day are not actual decisions, but habits. The habits grow stronger and stronger over time and become more and more automatic. So make sure you have developed the right habits. Habits are so powerful because they create neurological cravings.

The key to creating positive change for yourself is to make your desired actions into habits. The good news is that habits are not destiny. All habits can be ignored, changed, or replaced. But it is not easy because a habit never truly disappears, it is just replaced by new habit.

Habits of Successful People

1. Make Decisions And Take Action

Successful people are good at making decisions. They do not delay in making a decision and taking action. This does not mean they are taking irresponsible decisions, but sometimes it is essential to take a risk and follow our intuition and simply take action. It may not be perfect, but we keep on improvising and learning from our mistakes and correct accordingly. Mistakes and failures are part of the game. Most successful people fail more than they win, but they never shy away from taking decisions and actions.

2. Time Management

Becoming successful in anything in your life is greatly connected to how organized you are and how well you manage your time. All truly successful people are great at managing the time they have available in their hands. They make every moment count and they do not accept distractions or interruptions. They are exceptional planners and always try to stay organized.

3. Focus

Successful people focus on one thing at a time. They pick one thing and devote their time and energy to becoming great in that one area. Many of us take on too many goals at once and we end up distracted and ultimately frustrated with ourselves. Therefore, pick one big goal that is over and above your regular commitments and devote all of your time, efforts, energy, and attention to doing your best for that goal.

How To Build Good Habits

Experts say that the best way to form a new habit is to tie it to an existing habit. So, observe the patterns in your day and think about how you can use existing habits to create new, positive ones.

For many of us, our morning routine is our strongest routine, so that is a great place to attach a new habit. A morning cup of coffee, for example, can create a great opportunity to start a new one-minute meditation practice. Or, while you are brushing your teeth, immediately after you can start walking for five minutes.

Dr. B.J. Fogg, the author of the book "Tiny Habits," described that big behavior change requires a high level of motivation that often cannot be sustained. He suggested starting with tiny habits to make the new habit as easy as possible in the beginning. For example, a daily short walk could be the beginning of an exercise habit, or putting an apple in your bag every day could lead to better eating habits.

In his own life, Dr. Fogg started with just two push-ups a day and, to make the habit stick, tied his push-ups to a daily habit of going to the bathroom. He began after a bathroom trip doing two push-ups. Now he has a habit of 40 to 80 push-ups a day.

British researchers who published the study in the European Journal of Social Psychology showed that the amount of time it took for the task to become a habit ranged from 18 to 254 days. The median time was 66 days. The habits take a long time to create, but they form faster when you practice them more often, so start with something easy to do.

Habit researchers know people are more likely to form new habits when they clear away the obstacles that stand in their way.

Chapter Summary

To sum it up, success is like a seed that needs soil to germinate and grow. Habit is just like a good quality soil which helps to germinate the seed when combined with other supporting elements such as self-belief, discipline, hard work, actions, etc. Success is the feeling of fulfillment that you feel when you achieve your goal.

Florence Chadwick was the first woman to swim the English Channel in both directions. In 1952, at age 34, she decided to attempt the 26-mile swim between the California coastline and Catalina Island.

The sea was very chilled and icy and there was dense fog. Chadwick traveled with a team who were in boats and whose job was to keep an eye out for sharks and be prepared to assist in the event of an unexpected occurrence.

Alongside one of the boats, her mother and her trainer were offered encouragement when the goal is nearer. But all she could see was fog. They urged her not to quit. But with only a half-mile to go, she quit.

Two months later, she tried again. This time, despite the same dense fog, she swam with her faith intact and her goal pictured in her mind. She had a mental image of the shoreline in her mind as she pushed herself along.

Commitment toward your goal is the act of having a true passion for what it is you do. A great way to establish commitment and continuous improvement is to set daily goals for yourself. This gives you purpose, drive, ambition, and something to reach for daily. Your daily goals should be actionable and attainable so that at the end of the day, you feel accomplished and can experience that feeling of success.

Significance Of Commitment In Success

Each of us can set commitments to become successful.

1. Focus On Goal

The only thing you should be focused on is your future outcome. You should get rid of instant gratification by paying attention to the momentary pleasure. But you should stay away from these momentary pleasures and distractions.

2. Total Commitment

Successful goal achievement requires 100% commitment. It is always easy to make excuses, but it is very difficult to get back on track after those excuses. Once you have decided, stick to that, no room for any excuses or exceptions. True commitment is when you focus solely on your goal, not your distractions. It is your choice that if you want to reduce expenses, then you choose to spend less or as per your budget. If you want to be fit then you choose to do physical exercise daily. In short, once you decided on the desired future outcome, you remove all the distractions other than the choice and focus on what you are committed to.

3. Total Dedication

Hard work, commitment and dedication leads to a successful life and to the desired outcome. Stephen R. Covey in his book, "The 7 Habits of Highly Effective People" has rightly advised to "Begin with the end in mind." Your level of desire will determine your results.

4. Visualize Your Goal

Visualization is a powerful tool. Just visualize your desired outcome every day, morning and evening, for a moment. Just feel it and completely immerse yourself in the smells and sounds of the environment. When you can focus on the result instead of momentary temptation, you will make the right choices that support your desired outcome.

Seven Commitments To Success

1. Never Giving Up

Never giving up is the ultimate mantra to success. In your life journey, you will fall many times. You might also make mistakes and fail, and it is natural and happens to everyone.

To succeed and develop the attitude of never giving up, you have to have a lot of faith in yourself. This indomitable spirit will help you get through the tough times easier.

2. Taking Massive Action Every Day

You need to commit yourself to take massive action every single day without any excuses irrespective your goal is small or big. Be inspired enough to take massive action every day without any excuses.

3. Believing In Yourself

Most people underestimate their capabilities that prevent them to reach their true potential. Whatever you would like to achieve, make sure that you believe in it, and trust your abilities to accomplish it. First, you believe in yourself and then others will start believing in you.

Many successful people write their strengths, achievements in a notebook and read them aloud every morning. This little technique can do wonders to boost up your belief in yourself.

4. Learning Continually

Those who learn new things continually have an edge over others. People get satisfied once they achieve something and efforts get lesser later on. The zeal and enthusiasm diminish slowly. Continual learning is important to combat future challenges.

5. Say No

You will be attracted to do many other activities but if these are not aligned with your goals, you should learn to say "no" to prevent any distraction from your goal. It requires a lot of courage to say no to friends but doing it will make your life more successful and happier.

6. Be Ethical

Always be ethical towards the achievement of the goal. You might get inclined to the idea of doing something unethical and get quick results. However, such things always come with a price and can easily ruin everything within a flash. Remember that the journey to success is going to test your character along with dedication.

7. Maintaining Health

Your physical and mental health plays an important part in your life as everything directly or indirectly depends on it.

Do not work too hard so that you start ignoring your health. If you have worked tirelessly for straight 40 hours, it makes sense to give your body the rest it deserves. If you're working on weekends, try spending at least a few hours with your near and dear ones and recharge your batteries.

Chapter Summary

Staying committed to your goal is one of the most fundamental principles of success. Commitment entails dedication, the ability to work hard and bear infinite fortitude. Commitment toward achieving these long-term goals keeps an individual motivated. Commitment makes it imperative that one must abandon his comfort zone. It is a commitment that transforms the vision into reality. Being committed thus requires that a person is full efforts in his endeavors and remains persistent enough to achieve success. So, when the commitment is high, all other success elements such as willpower, focus and hardworking, etc. automatically aligned to convert a dream into reality.

"Gratitude for the present moment and the fullness of life now is the true prosperity."—Eckhart Tolle

Anthony Ray Hinton spent thirty years on death row for a crime he did not commit. He was convicted in two cases and he was sent to jail.

As he was on death row, which meant that he was held in solitary confinement for nearly three decades in a five-by-seven-foot cell, allowed out only one hour a day. During prison, he was supported by his mother's unwavering faith in his innocence, as well as that of a longtime friend, Lester Bailey, who visited him monthly. But, Hinton quickly became a friend and counselor to other inmates and the death row guards, many of whom begged Hinton's attorney to get him out.

The Supreme Court of the United States ordered in a unanimous decision for his release and he was able to walk free. In an interview he was quoted saying:

"One does not know the value of freedom until it is taken away, People run out of the rain. I run into the rain... I am so grateful for every drop. Just to feel it on my face."

Hinton was later interviewed on 60 Minutes. The interviewer asked if he was angry at the people who put him in jail. He said he forgave them all.

The interviewer asked, "But they took thirty years of your life—how can you not be angry?"

Hinton responded, "If I'm angry and unforgiving, they will have taken the rest of my life."

Hinton is a strong example of the ability to respond with joy and gratitude despite horrendous circumstances.

Success Starts With Gratitude

Gratitude and success are virtually inseparable. Gratitude increases social relationships, boosts careers, or businesses by helping to improve your success in critical areas. Gratitude is one habit that improves your happiness, lowers stress, improves health, enriches relationships, and even has a positive effect on business and career. Perhaps no other habit can have so great an impact on your well-being.

Some of the most admired people in the world faced tremendous hardship for a long period of their life.

- Mahatma Gandhi was sentenced to six years in prison after organizing a non-violent protest that turned violent. Gandhi was eventually horrified by the violence, yet he served his sentence and continued to inspire people.

- Nelson Mandela served twenty-seven years in prison. But he used that long period to develop his mind and character. Imagine what mental battle he passed through and what attitude of perseverance he exercised.

- Martin Luther King was arrested twenty-six times during the fight for equality.

- Walt Disney endured failure time after time early in his career before finally achieving a breakthrough.

- Helen Keller was the first deaf-blind person to earn a Bachelor of Arts degree. She learned to appreciate, and accomplished more than most, despite not being able to see or hear from the age of two.

- Lance Armstrong after battling cancer launched the LiveStrong foundation that provides support for people affected by the cancer movement.

The list can go on and on. If we are not able to keep hope, accept what is, and experience gratitude, it is hard to move forward.

Benefits Of Gratitude

- Gratitude increases determination, willpower, enthusiasm, and focus, so productivity improves and achieves more.

- Gratitude helps people to become more social and strengthen relationships. It encourages social behavior while discouraging disruptive behavior.

- Grateful people are highly focused and energetic and not easily burnt out. The moral of the grateful people are always high.

- Gratitude increases commitment and emotional well-being and leads to reduce stress.

- People who express gratitude are more conscientious, agreeable, open, and extrovert.

- Grateful people sleep better leading to greater energy and optimism. They are more resilient to trauma.

- Gratitude reduces symptoms of illness, lowers blood pressure, and strengthens the immune system. Grateful people are less depressed.

- Gratitude increases work efficiency and makes fast progress.

- Gratitude increases productivity by increasing confidence and decreasing insecurity.

- Gratitude helps people stay focused on their work or goals as they are less likely to be distracted by worries.

- Gratitude increases self-esteem which enables successful people to take necessary risks and accept failure as a learning experience easier.

- Gratitude helps your network to get mentors and benefactors.

How To Practice Gratitude?

Many people, when they see someone happy and successful, they just get annoyed, they feel envy and jealous. But there is a way out and the key is gratitude.

With the simple act of acknowledging a few things you are grateful for, you become more open to recognizing these moments as they happen throughout the day.

Becoming more grateful means shifting your mindset to one that embraces positivity. And changing your mindset doesn't happen overnight. Luckily, there are some scientifically proven methods of practicing gratitude and adding joy to your life.

- Keep a diary: Keeping a gratitude diary helps to transform your mindset from pessimistic to optimistic. Just note down three grateful things for the day before sleep, along with the reasons.

- Practice mindfulness: Once you start practicing mindfulness throughout the day, you will be more grateful for many things and your gratitude will improve.

- Make gratitude a priority in your life: Making gratitude a priority, you transform your life to a larger extent by improving your gratitude very fast.

- Smile: Smile is priceless. It does not require any effort. Still many cannot smile. Practicing to smile spreads positivity and improves gratitude.

When you are depressed and pessimistic about your life, it is practically difficult to think positive thoughts and practice gratitude. But when you are depressed, you should reflect on past struggles and remember how you overcame them. Such things help to remind yourself that you are capable to take any challenge. Many people counter every negative thought with a positive thought.

Chapter Summary

Practicing gratefulness allows you to capture the full essence of life every moment. Gratitude can lead to an increase in determination, energy, enthusiasm, and achievement. Gratitude helps people to feel more positive emotions, relish good experiences, improve their health, deal with adversity, and build strong relationships.

Overall in this chapter, you have learned the methodology to improve gratitude.

Success requires more than talent. While talent and knowledge are essential, the key that unlocks them both is attitude.

This book has covered eight broad attitudinal aspects, viz., self-belief, sacrifices, perseverance, action-oriented, ownership, creating habits, commitment, and gratitude that play a very important role in creating the required mindset and building the foundation for success.

Self-belief is the basics of any success. Even the highest talented and hardworking person does not succeed in absence of any self-belief. In the third chapter, the book has covered the details of self-belief, why they are so important, how it can be improved to make the foundation strong.

Sacrifice is an important aspect of success that has covered in Chapter 4. It is said that every human being has to pay the price for success. This chapter described the impact of sacrifices and its role in success.

The mind has the power to control everything in our life. Practicing perseverance is the area where everybody needs to focus on. People do not succeed mostly due to a lack of perseverance. It helps to get some control over the never-give-up attitude and willpower at every stage of life. This chapter has given the outline of perseverance and the method of practicing this.

Action is the key component of any success. It is essential to make timely action a habit. Our attitude plays a big part in our everyday lives and shapes our future. By taking action, our attitude develops towards success.

In the next chapter, the book has described the importance of taking ownership of success by accelerating the process of achieving the goals and makes the journey of the person most memorable.

The topic covered in the next chapter is the whole and sole of any success. The attitude of creating a habit is the foundation of any success at any level. All successful people have one thing in common and that is creating good habits. All other things start from this point only.

Commitment is a very powerful driver when applied to the purpose. Commitment gives you purpose, drive, ambition, and something to reach for daily. The stronger the commitment is, the bigger is the success.

Gratitude and success are virtually inseparable. Gratitude increases social capital and improves relationships and keeps the mind energetic. Chapter 10 has described the importance of gratitude, benefits of gratitude, and the method of practicing gratitude.

In a nutshell, your attitude determines your success and failure. Firstly, you make your attitude—then your attitude will make or break you. Everyone hits brick walls in their life. When faced with adversity, you can either decide to climb the wall, creating a tunnel under the wall, break through the wall, or sit there and blame your upbringing as the reason for staying where you are. The choice is yours!!! You can continue to reside with low self-esteem and a negative attitude or create a positive new future for yourself.

May I Ask You For A Small Favor?

At the outset, I would like to thank you for taking out time to read this book. You could have chosen any other book, but you took mine, and I totally appreciate this.

I hope you got at least a few actionable insights that will have a positive impact on your life.

I'd love it if you could leave a review of the book. Reviews may not matter to big-name authors; but these are a tremendous help for authors like me, who don't have much following.

I sincerely request you to leave your review by clicking the below link, it will directly lead you to the book review page.

DIRECT REVIEW LINK

Thanks for your support of my work.

Disclaimer

Although the publisher and the author have made every effort to ensure that the information in this book is correct, and while this publication is designed to provide accurate information regarding the subject matter covered, the publisher and the author assume no responsibility for errors, inaccuracies, omissions, or any other inconsistencies herein and hereby disclaim any liability to any party for any loss, damage, or disruption caused by errors or omissions, whether such errors or omissions result from negligence, accident, or any other cause.

The ideas, procedures, and suggestions contained in this book are not intended as a substitute for consulting with an expert. Neither the author nor the publisher shall be liable or responsible for any loss or damage allegedly arising from any information or suggestion in this book.

Names, characters, and incidents in this book are either the product of the author's imagination or used in a fictitious manner. Any resemblance to an actual person, living or dead, or actual events is purely coincidental.

Gratitude

This book is dedicated to my spouse, Sutapa whose continuous support and inspiration help me to continue on the writer's journey.

I sincerely thank all my readers, who inspired me with their love and appreciation for my first two books.

About the Author

Pradip N Das is an author, mentor, and professional who looks beyond the existing challenges to find the solution for the future. While he has been an avid reader for more than a decade, the idea of writing a book came to him in 2020.

Personal development is his niche, and he commenced his writing journey with "Success Strategy for Students", which was published in September 2020 to an overwhelming response, hitting the #1 best-seller on Amazon. The "Seven Essential Skills for Success" is the second book also achieved Amazon's #1 bestseller. This book "The Power of Attitude in Success" is the third book in the series for which the author has planned for more additions. The author can be contacted at jnjbd1024@gmail.com.

This is the third book of the series "Success Plan for Students". The details of the other two books are given below:-

Book 1:

Success Strategy for Students

"Success Strategy for Students" is the powerful solution to achieve your goals, skyrocket your productivity, master success strategy, and skills.

This book provides a concise guideline for the strategy to be adopted to improve the student's foundation toward success from an early age.

CLICK HERE

Book 2

Seven Essential Skills for Success

Life is a journey. In this beautiful journey, people travel with different traits, some with sports, some with teaching, some with social services, but ultimately every person reaches a destination, knowingly or unknowingly. This book has covered seven essential skills: public speaking, writing, analytical, problem-solving, negotiation, leadership, and decision-making. These skills are important to create the foundation for success in life and very much significant for everybody, especially for students who are trying to build the foundation of their future.

CLICK HERE